SAWYER, KID LAWYER

PLAYGROUND DEBATE

Written By:
Shanene Muldrow

Illustrated By:
Sheldon Muldrow

For Publishing Information, contact Journal Joy at:
Info@thejournaljoy.com
www.thejournaljoy.com

Paperback ISBN: 9781957751870

Hardcover ISBN: 9781957751016

Ebook ISBN: 9798349294808
Editor: Khalia Kai Tarver
First edition, 2025

This Book Belongs To:

_____

Dedicated to our aunts, uncles, cousins, and families that helped to mold us.

Ok Children, it's time for recess.

Enjoy your break, Ms. Butler said as she headed back inside 44 Elementary.

Wait, the slide is empty.

Children what is wrong, Ms. Butler states.

Rose and I saw that the slide was free. We ran over to the slide, and at the same time, they ran over to the slide.

Ok, says Ms. Butler.

We got here first, Rose states. No, they did not, Gavin yells back.

Ms. Butler states, "Whoa, Children, recess is over so no one will slide today".

Sawyer whispers to Rose, we need to come up with a plan for recess tomorrow.

We're going to get to the slide before anyone else.

How do you **plan** to do that, Rose asks.

I'll **figure** it out tonight, Sawyer replies.

Mom and Dad, I have a question, Sawyer asks.

What's wrong sweetie, Mom replies.

During recess, Rose and I ran towards the slide, but at the same time, Gavin and Eddie ran towards it and got to the slide before us.

Scout jokingly says, that's because girls are slower than boys.

Dad says young men are supposed to allow young ladies to slide first.

Exactly, Mom joins in.

Ms. Butler says, Ok class, have fun at recess.

Sawyer and Rose rush to the door to head outside followed by Eddie and Gavin.

Aww man, Sawyer yells out.

Ha ha, boys win again,
Gavin jokes.

This isn't fair; we should be able to use the slide. Listen to what my dad said to me last night at dinner.

Sawyer plays the recording – "Young men are supposed to allow young ladies to slide first."

Your dad has a point, but not today and probably not tomorrow, Jason says with a laugh.

How did everything go today during **recess**? Dad asked.

Not as planned, but I think I need to meet with Gavin tomorrow and discuss a **better** way to share the slide.

Sounds like a **plan** to me, Mom says.

Good night.

Let's **discuss** the slide.

Gavin laughs, you probably won't get to it **before** us today.

Yes, we should split the days, Sawyer states.

Split no, whoever get's there first, which will be the boys can use the slide.

Have you heard of sharing?; Sawyer asks.

Yes, it's something my parents make me do with my older brother.

Monday	Tuesday	Wednesday	Thursday	Friday

TIME ON SLIDE

Great, I made us a **chart**. The **girls** can use the slide on Mondays and Wednesdays.

G   B   G   B

OPEN

The **boys** are on Tuesdays and Thursdays.

Friday we **share**.

I have to discuss this with the rest of the boys, Gavin says.

Ok, let me know by lunch.

So has a decision been made,
Sawyer asks Gavin.

Yes, we agree, Gavin says
with a smile.

Great, I just need you to
sign the schedule.

Everyone cheers.

Anything interesting happen in school today, Mom asks.

We made a map of the United States out of play-doh. I'm halfway done, Scout states.

I can't wait to see that, Dad tells Scout.

It's for back-to-school night, so you will definitely see it, Scout states.

Great, says Dad.

What about you Sawyer, any *luck* on the playground debate, Dad asks?

I had a good talk with Gavin before we started our lessons this morning, Sawyer said.

All of the boys accepted an offer to share the slide every other day!

I knew you would be able to come up with a solution, Mom stated.

Ok, that's one win for the girls kinda, Scout says jokingly.

And many *more* to come, Sawyer says with a smirk.

The Creators of Sawyer, Kid Lawyer

Shanene E. Muldrow is the author behind Sawyer, Kid Lawyer. This series is loosely based on her childhood and experiences growing up in Teaneck, New Jersey. In her professional life, she drives effectiveness and efficiency, through project management and communications.

During her downtime, she uses her creativity to develop celebratory experiences for her family and friends and jots down new story ideas for this series.

She is available for speaking engagements and may be contacted via email: at Sawyerkidlawyer@gmail.com.

Website: https://sawyerkidlawyer.com

Shanene E. Muldrow, Author

The Creators of Sawyer, Kid Lawyer

Sheldon B. Muldrow, Shanene's older brother, graduated from Temple University with a Bachelor of Arts in Biology and Fine Arts minor in 2003. Later obtaining his doctorate in podiatric medicine in 2010. While maintaining a career as a healthcare provider, he continues to follow his interests in the arts. He spends some of his spare time drawing in a sketchbook and painting still life.

Sheldon enjoys quality time with family, as much as possible, and is an avid sports fanatic.
Website: https://sawyerkidlawyer.com

Sheldon B. Muldrow, Illustrator